What *Real* Landlords *Know*

by Linda Grischy

Contents

This book is dedicated to
my husband Scott
and my sons, Dereck and Dustan
for all the years and endless labor
they have invested in rental properties

and
with affection and gratitude to my writing group
for the many hours of support and inspiration they have given me
in writing this book

and
with admiration and appreciation
to my friend Judy Bobrow,
whose endless patience and incredible attention to detail
in editing, helped make this book easier to read

and
many thanks to all the wonderful friends and family
who have shared their incredible stories and experience.

Without all of these wonderful people this book could not have
been written, and many landlords would have to suffer the
consequences of not having this insight in advance.

Introduction

Welcome to the World of Rental Real Estate

Ever dream of becoming a real estate tycoon - owning dozens of properties and raking in thousands of dollars monthly? Maybe you just want to rent out a house or two, generate a little extra income, and build your nest egg? Either way, read on. This book is designed to help you achieve your goals by understanding what you need to know about rental property. Through the stories of many landlords you can learn what works, the pitfalls to avoid and the ways in which you can achieve your dreams more quickly!

Whether you are planning to own several rental properties or one, keep in mind that if you don't want to lose money, you will need to treat this as a business. The decision to purchase rental property as a means of generating income means doing some math. It means putting together a budget and estimating costs just as any other business would require. In fact putting together a business plan is a good idea. If you plan on going to a bank or an investor for financing, you will want a business plan and a projected profit and loss statement. In the back of this book you will find a business plan specifically for rental property (Appendix A) an example of a Profit & Loss Statement (Appendix B) and a sample Cash Flow Projection (Appendix C). There also are some interesting statistics and tidbits at the end of the book (Appendix D) you might find useful.

If you want to be an effective landlord, you will need to find a balance between being a nice person and taking care of yourself and your own financial responsibilities. You'll need to determine when to do things yourself and when to hire experts. You'll need to evaluate tenants to find a good match for your property. You'll need to think about issues like pets, difficult neighbors, non-payment of rent and much more. I have written this book to help you prepare for the many challenges you will face. Included are those things I have learned through my own experience, as well as what I have learned from others in the landlord business.

Chapter 1

Home Sweet Home

Renting out your house instead of selling it is a great way to survive a bad seller's market. There is a big difference, however, between renting out a house that you previously considered "home" and renting out a house you purchased with the intent of leasing it to someone else. You put love, time, energy and sweat equity into your own home to make it a wonderful retreat: the expensive bathroom vanity, mosaic tiles and the special window treatments that match your beloved carpeting with the thick pad. Yes, you have added many of the finer amenities to your own home.

I remember the feeling I had returning to my first home after a few years of renting it out. The yard I'd spent so many hours nurturing had gone wild. Few flowers remained and the feral shrubs were completely unmanageable. The house itself looked run down, even though we tried to maintain it as best we could. The fine amenities were now broken, cracked, chipped or dented. Of course you have a security deposit that covers any damages. Many of the small incidentals are easily overlooked, however, when you do your walk-through to determine if any damage has been done. You don't notice the scratch in the counter, the cracked tile in the shower, little dents here and there in the doorways. But over time you see that the place doesn't look like it did when you lived there. In fact you barely recognize it as the same house you once knew and loved. For me, it was heartbreaking to see my once pretty little home turned into just an ordinary "rental" house.

Even if you purchase a property as an investment, don't be surprised to see a change in the character of the home after renting it out for a few years. You should plan on putting a little zest back into the house now and then. Inexpensive improvements to keep it looking nice and updated will pay off in the long run.

Checklist

⌂ If you are planning on purchasing rental property for profit, have you completed a Rental Business Plan, and Projected Profit and Loss Statement?

⌂ Have you planned for future sprucing up expenses?

Chapter 2

Catching Quality Tenants

Getting a good tenant is the **most** important aspect of renting out your property. There are so many great renters looking for good property and you want the best tenant. The first step is to make sure your property is as attractive as you can make it without spending your life savings. Next, you want to match the right tenant to the home. If you have a good match, the tenants will stay longer and complain less, saving you money and future headaches!

Inexperienced renters may expect a house rental to be like renting an apartment. They even may think of you, their landlord, as Mom and Pop #2. We've had tenants who expect us to change a light bulb, move their furniture and many other things they should or could easily do themselves. Unless you are willing to hold their hands 24/7 for the entire length of the lease, it is a good idea to let them know up front what is expected of them. And you should include that information in the lease.

Additionally you should be aware that there are some deceptive renters out there. Because most small landlords do not report these fraudulent tenants, it is difficult for an inexperienced landlord to know when and how they are being deceived. These tenants move from one rental property to another paying little or no rent. They often have no job, no assets and no forwarding address, so it is difficult to ever recoup your losses. How does their operation work?

These dishonest folks may or may not have phony IDs. They will provide you with contact information for their previous landlords and employers, who always give them a very favorable reference. The problem is, it will actually be their friends pretending to be an employer or landlord. They may have stellar credit checks, because the money owed to past landlords has never been reported. They know it is rare that they would ever be criminally charged, making this a lucrative enterprise for them.

From experience the con artists know how many months it takes for the eviction process; They've been through it before. And because they have no job and no assets they have nothing that can be taken away and nothing to lose. Few landlords or property mangers are aware of this form of fraud and are not prepared for it. This enables swindlers to go from one innocent landlord to another.

How can you protect yourself from these scams? Although you will have to decide what works best for you, here are a few ideas you can use:

- Make sure prospective tenants complete the **entire** rental application and sign it.
- Do a background check including criminal check.
- Get a credit report. (Remember, however, that the credit check may not reflect money owed to other landlords.)
- Do an internet search of the prospective tenant's name, cell phone number, driver's license number, previous addresses, references, and other rental application information.
- Check the following links:
  http://www.NoPayTenants.com/
  http://www.RipOffReport.com/
  http://www.AngiesList.com/

In addition, when contacting previous landlords, don't tell them initially that you are seeking a reference. Instead ask about available rental units. If they are not landlords, you may catch them off guard. When contacting a listed employer, check the internet for a phone number to contact the business rather than using the number on the application.

Yes, you'll need to do your homework. If you don't you could end up like one of my family members. She rented her house to someone who seemed to be very nice. After the first month he called to say he couldn't pay the rent because his young child had been sick. She felt sorry for him and let that month's rent slide. The following month he called to say he was having problems with his job and his boss. Then he called to tell them the house was haunted. He'd had to do an exorcism on it because his two-year-old child had seen some strange things! He eventually moved out owing well over $3,000. My family member admitted to not having checked the tenant out prior to renting to him.

Finding the right tenant is a very important part of being a successful landlord. You will save time and money by finding a tenant who is a good fit for what you are offering. If the house is too small, too far from their work, or doesn't have a particular feature, such as a garage or basement, they will likely move out before their lease is up. Every time a tenant moves out you will need to inspect, make repairs and return deposits. You often need to hire someone to clean or spend the time to do it yourself. And when you property is vacant, you lose rental income.

There are many suggestions out there for finding a good tenant. Some work especially well if you have dozens of people looking at your property daily and can choose between hundreds of possible renters. However, a more likely scenario is that you are under pressure to fill your vacancy soon.

So how do you know who is the right tenant for your home? The short and simple answer is – you don't. There are ways during the selection process, however, that can help you decide. Throughout my years as a landlord I have interviewed hundreds of prospective tenants and met their children, pets and significant others. During that time I've developed my own strategy for choosing tenants.

Screen First

You can begin with the phone call before setting up a meeting at the house. I try to understand what a prospective tenant is looking for and what they feel is important in the place they live. For example, I may ask how many people will be living there. If the house is small, I let them know this right away. If they are looking for a short term lease, I let them know that I'm looking for a one year lease. After that, I usually suggest that the person drive by the property first to see if they like the neighborhood and the house. This saves me endless hours and fuel in showing a home that is not even close to what the prospective tenant had in mind. I also make sure to get their name and phone number when setting up an appointment. That way I'm less likely to be stood up.

Using Applications Effectively

Using an application allows you to collect the information you will need to qualify prospective tenants. The application I use includes information on employment and other sources of income. I get their employer's name and phone number so I can verify that they are in fact working. I also ask for contact information of previous landlords. There is really no point in calling current landlords because if the tenant

12

is bad, the landlord will be so happy to get rid of them that he or she will likely be less than honest. The previous landlord, however, may share some valuable information with you. Please be careful and find out the laws in your state regarding what you can and cannot ask. Keep this law in mind as well when you get a call regarding your own tenants!

The application should also inquire about pets, the number of vehicles and type of equipment a prospective tenant may want to keep on the premises, emergency information, possible bankruptcy situations, co-applicants, and references. I've had tenants with a part-time landscaping business park all kinds of equipment on the lawn and in the driveway. Knowing and having an understanding about such things prior to move-in is always best!

Many landlords require a credit check and this may be a good idea if you are unsure about the candidates you are considering or are new at property rentals. It may also depend on the area in which you live. I do not *always* require credit checks. However, I do let a potential tenant know that I am interested in finding someone who will take good care of the house and pay the rent on time. I emphasize that I am trying to pay my bills and hope the house will appreciate in value over time. You'd be surprised how many people feel that their landlords are only trying to make a fortune from them! Letting my tenants know up front what is most important to me (covering my costs and keeping the place looking good) helps them better understand what is expected of them.

During the application process I ask a lot of questions and spend time just trying to get to know a prospective tenant. I review the application while talking to them and ask for clarification on a number of things. It is amazing what people reveal to you when you are talking to them as one person to another. I've had potential renters tell me they were in the process of suing their current landlord as well as other people. I've also had people tell me they made incredible sums of money, which made me wonder, "Why would you want to rent this house if you have that much money?" If their story seems too good to be true, it often is.

A number of people I've interviewed have confessed that they had to file for bankruptcy in the past. I've rented to many of them anyway. Every one of these tenants turned out to be an excellent renter! Sometimes people go through hard times; they may not have had control over their situation. And sometimes a person who shows up in a new car, wearing smart new clothes and expensive jewelry may seem like a great possibility, but may be headed toward financial crisis. Oftentimes, someone who has previously filed bankruptcy has learned how to better manage their money!

A suggestion that was passed on to me years ago is that you should drive by the prospective tenant's current address. You can tell a lot about someone by seeing where and how they live. If you can't drive by, try looking them up on Google maps - street view. I used this suggestion after meeting with a very nice man who was quite interested in renting our property. We were having a lovely discussion when he let it slip that he loved watching shows like *Storage Wars* and enjoyed buying and reselling all kinds of things on ebay. My mind suddenly filled with pictures from the TV show *Hoarders*. I quickly made note of his address and drove by. Fortunately he only enjoyed the show; he wasn't living it!

After showing a house to several prospective tenants, and losing rent while making mortgage payments from his or her personal savings account, a landlord will begin to feel desperate to find a renter. That is a prescription for trouble.

A good friend of mine had been feeling exactly that way. After her current tenant moved out, she spent extra time and money to make the house look especially nice before looking for a new tenant. The timing wasn't good and she was growing concerned about finding a renter when a couple showed up ready to move in. While sensing that they were less than the ideal tenants, she decided to ignore her instincts and accept them anyway. Within six months they were unable to pay their rent.

After her notices were ignored she contacted an attorney, who prepared the case for court. The tenants showed up with their legal aid attorneys, who requested all of the maintenance records and move-in and move-out forms from the last five years. Assuming she would never collect, even if she won the judgment, my friend decided to settle for possession of the home. The judge granted the tenants 30 additional days to move out.

After the tenants vacated, she was very disturbed by the condition of the house. Shocked by all the junk they left behind, she found it difficult to even make her way through the various rooms. Meat had been removed from the freezer and left under some of the junk. It wasn't found until the smell became foul. The odor from dog and cat feces and urine permeated the house.

There are two lessons to keep in mind from this incident. First, follow your instincts, and second, try to hold out for the right tenant.

One of the best ways to attract good tenants is to offer a home that is clean and well maintained. I cannot tell you how many times I've heard from prospective tenants that my property was the cleanest and in the best condition of any they had seen. It may cost a little more to keep your rental unit in good shape, but in the long run having a great tenant pays for itself. If you have a great property to offer prospects will fight over renting your property!

Finally, a very important lesson I have learned over the years is that most people, when treated fairly, will treat you the same way. I try to follow the Golden Rule by treating my tenants as I would want to be treated. And I expect the same of them.

Checklist

☐ Do you plan to check references, credit, background and/or criminal records?

☐ Have you considered driving by a prospective tenant's current home?

☐ Do you have a list of potential questions to ask your prospective tenants?

☐ Do you plan to share with your tenants what is important to you?

☐ Is your property in good condition and clean enough to attract the best tenants?

☐ Are you prepared emotionally and financially for the possibility of a long-term vacancy?

⌂ Do you know the property rental laws in your area?

Chapter 3

Here's Looking at You, Lease

I've used a number of different leases over the years; some that are written in very formal legal jargon and others that are much easier to understand. In the beginning, when I needed a lease, I simply picked one up at the nearest office supply store. My tenants and I glanced over it and then we all signed it. And that worked OK for a time. But after a while I realized that my lease did not address certain issues. And in addition *I couldn't understand it.* So I began searching for a lease that better fit my style. I want to understand what I'm signing, and I want my tenants to know what I'm asking of them. Fortunately I discovered that the Internet offers a wide selection of lease agreements. You can download them and make changes to accommodate your particular needs.

I've heard from other sources, however, that these non-conventional leases may not be enough. This is something you should discuss with your attorney and make sure you are using a lease that will hold up in court.

Whether you decide to use a pre-printed form lease, develop your own, or put something together with your attorney, here are some things you may want to include or consider:

Lawn Care - What is included and what is the tenant's responsibility. For example, who provides the lawn mower and who shovels the snow.

Repairs - Tenants should know that it is their responsibility to pay for any minor damages *they or their guests cause*. It is important to have this in the lease to avoid problems later on.

Garbage - Who pays for trash removal. Sometimes it is worth paying for it yourself to ensure that it doesn't pile up.

Utilities - Who pays for utilities. If you have to pay for water, consider covering the cost yourself and including it in the rent. If a tenant leaves owing water fees, the homeowner will usually be held responsible for the payment regardless of whose name is on the bill. If you plan on having the tenant pay the water bill, make sure to include it in the lease.

Paint - Make sure the tenant knows that any painting they want to do must be approved by you first. Agree on the colors.

Pets - If you allow them, have the type and names of the pets included in the lease. Be sure to put in a clause that no additional pets can be added without your consent. If you charge for pets, be sure to include this information as well.

Additional Residents - Consider using a clause addressing who is permitted to live on the premises including any extended family.

Hazardous, Dangerous or Inflammable Materials - Having to pay to remove hazardous materials after a tenant moves out can be expensive and could cause many problems later on.

Inspection - You want to be able to inspect your property from time-to-time. Be sure your lease has a provision for inspections.

Termination - Some leases are *fixed-term* and end on a certain date without further action. Others may include a provision that the lease becomes a *month-to-month* after a future date. Some leases assign a condition that the rent will increase by a specific percentage or dollar amount after the termination date.

One very cold winter day in late January, we received a call from some young tenants indicating a problem with the pipes. "I think the pipes froze and we have a leak," he said. "I can hear water. I think it's coming from under the house."

We'd owned the house for more than 12 years and never had a problem before. I knew there was good insulation so was very surprised with the news. I quickly called my plumber. He wasn't available so I began looking for another.

I was very fortunate to find a plumber who could get to the house quickly. He located the leaky pipe in the crawl space under the house. "I've found four leaks," he informed me over the phone.

"Wow, four? Yes, yes please fix them," I said, still trying to figure out what could have caused the problem. It had been a very cold winter but this was one house in which the pipes had never frozen!

About an hour later I received another call from the plumber. He'd found six more leaks. Two hours after that he'd found more. Finally he called to say he'd fixed over a dozen leaks.

"I can't believe it," the plumber began. "Those kids went away for a week's vacation and turned the furnace off! In the middle of the winter, they turned the heat completely off and left!" He was appalled. I was shocked. Apparently they thought they would save money by not having to heat the house while they were out of town.

For the next two weeks the plumber returned to the house for newly sprung leaks in the pipes. Finally he sent me the bill. There were 24 broken pipes in all. Some of the pipes were hard to get at and the walls had to be cut open to reach them. So not only was there a gigantic plumbing bill, there were huge holes in the walls that needed to be repaired.

The tenants did not want to pay for the plumber or for having the walls repaired. I pointed to the lease, which showed they were responsible for any damage they caused to the house. I was grateful for having a lease that had this language. In the end they forfeited their deposit, which covered most, but not all, of the expense.

One landlord I know permitted her tenants to allow extended family members to move in. The mother of the tenant became romantically involved with a married neighbor. Soon a battle of revenge ensued. Fights erupted and windows were broken along with other damage to the rental house. The police were called on several occasions and finally the tenants were forced to leave. If there had been a clause stating something to the effect that only those listed on the lease may live on the premises, and that any additional occupants would require written permission, this unfortunate situation could have been prevented.

A clause regarding hazardous materials can also be included in a lease. Consider this situation that occurred in Easthampton, Massachusetts. Nearly half of a street had to be blocked off and people evacuated by police and firefighters for an hour and a half. A hazardous materials crew came in to investigate a suspicious liquid that was left behind by an evicted tenant. Apparently the tenant had been extracting metals from computer chips, leaving behind a corrosive liquid acid in the basement. The material was capable of causing skin burns and if stored improperly, exploding. The landlord was fortunate that the dangerous material was discovered quickly and that no one was injured.

As a landlord, the lease is your most valuable tool. It may protect you from any number of possible problems. Be sure to go over it carefully and check to make sure it complies with the law so that it will be your friend when needed. And make sure your tenants understand the lease and know and agree to what is expected of them.

Checklist

Have you checked over your lease carefully so that you know what it says?

Have you gone over the lease with the tenant so he or she understands their responsibilities?

Does your lease have a "RIGHT OF INSPECTION" clause?

Do you have a checklist your tenants can use to report the condition of the property when they move in?

Chapter 4

Know the Rules, Play by the Rules

There are a number of rules regarding leasing properties and they are not all from the government. Of course we know that the home needs to be in good repair, and we always want to offer our tenants a safe and healthy environment. We want to be legal. We want to be compliant with all regulations. You may discover that there are a number of rules you hadn't considered. For example, there are some municipalities that require owners to register their rental homes and will send an inspector to ensure the property meets code.

Sometimes regulations are imposed by another entity. A potential tenant informed us she had a small business and occasionally would need to meet with clients at the home. It seemed like a fair request, and I had no problem with it. However a few months later I was talking with a friend who happens to be an insurance agent. He informed me that most rental insurance policies do not cover you if someone is conducting business on the premises. Ask your insurance agent about what is covered or not covered each time you change policies. You may also want to review your policy every few years, as insurance policies can change without your knowledge. Many rental policies do not cover wood burners or trampolines. If these items are found on your property, your policy can be cancelled.

One final note regarding insurance, your rental property insurance doesn't cover your tenant's belongings. It is a good idea to make sure your tenants are aware of this so that they can purchase their own insurance if desired. This way they won't be upset with you if there is a problem.

I read an article in the local paper, "Landlord accused of discriminating," and my curiosity caused me to read more. It seems a landlord of a small cottage was approached by a woman wanting to rent from him. Her credit and references checked out and the landlord agreed to rent to her. However, after learning that the woman had two children, he informed her the home was too small for three people. The woman sued for discrimination. I include this because it is important to know the laws upfront and save yourself many dollars in legal fees in the future. As the owner, you may feel you have the right to choose your tenant. In this case, however, the tenant won the case. It is important to know and follow the law.

Not long ago our local news channel aired a story about a tenant who was being evicted for non-payment of rent. The tenant had refused to pay the rent because he had found bedbugs and wanted his landlord to eradicate them. Although the landlord provided bug bombs, bed bugs are very difficult to eradicate. A small apartment complex will likely have to spend $3,000 or more per unit to eliminate the pesky insects. In the end the landlord lost his case and shelled out more than $12,000 to an exterminator, not to mention the cost of the lawyer.

Every state has several important laws relating to rental property that are worthwhile to investigate and study. The following are some common issues addressed by these laws in most, but not all, states in the country.

- The dollar amount you are permitted to charge for late rent
- The dollar amount you are permitted to charge for bounced rent checks
- The dollar amount you are permitted to collect for security deposits
- Interest payments received on security deposits
- The deadline for returning security deposits
- The type of itemized statement required for security deposit deductions
- The notice you are required to give the tenant to enter the property
- Extenuating circumstances permitting the landlord to enter rental property
- Disclosures such as the presence of environmental hazards like mold

A young couple showed up to look at our rental property. They were excited at the prospect of renting a house because they had been living in a duplex for the past year. They had a lot of questions and we discussed responsibilities. They told me about some of the problems they'd encountered with their current landlord. It seems the furnace had gone out and the landlord was in no hurry to fix it. It was February, a cold month in Michigan. And although this young couple had been OK, staying with family on the colder nights, it was the story about their neighbors that has remained in my memory for some time.

As I said, they lived in a duplex. Another couple lived on the other side. After several days of no heat, and numerous calls to the landlord, the tenants decided to start a campfire in the living room.

I don't know what happened to either the landlord or the young couple who just wanted to stay warm. But I do know that it is a landlord's duty to immediately take care of any problem that is a health issue. As a landlord you need to know the rules and play by the rules!

Another important addition to your lease is an inventory checklist. This can be given to your tenant with the lease. You may require the tenant to return the checklist within the first seven days of moving in. When the tenant moves out, you will use this same list to determine what if any damage may have occurred during the tenant's tenancy and what was pre-existing.

With so many laws and so much at stake, having a good attorney you can call on is a great asset for any landlord. In fact laws can vary not only from state to state, but also from municipality to municipality. Your attorney can help you sort through these laws and save grief and money down the road.

Checklist

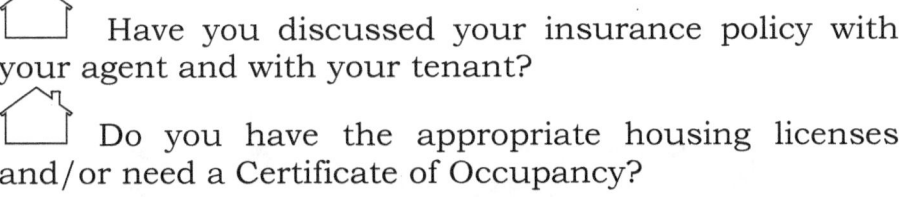

Have you discussed your insurance policy with your agent and with your tenant?

Do you have the appropriate housing licenses and/or need a Certificate of Occupancy?

☐ Have you studied the laws regarding landlord/tenant rights in your state?

☐ Are there local ordinances and do you know how they relate to rental property?

☐ Do you have an attorney you can contact to learn the laws and call on when you have questions?

☐ Do you have an inventory/property condition checklist to provide your tenant, and have you included the requirements in your lease?

Chapter 5

Color, Color Everywhere

Tenants often want to repaint your rental property with their preferred paint and colors. You might think it is great to have someone else do the painting for you, saving you time and money. But you may be in for a big surprise when you see the finished product. Not everyone appreciates the same color schemes. Additionally, not everyone who paints a room is an artist or a skilled painter. We learned the hard way that it's not always a good idea to allow tenants to paint your rental without at least consulting you and agreeing on the colors.

We lived in another state for a few years and while we were there we purchased a duplex. After moving back to Michigan we were happy to have found tenants for both units. One side was rented to a nice family who seemed quite happy to be there. But after a year they decided to move out. Our friend went over to inspect the place after they'd gone and assess any damage. The place was in relatively good shape, she reported, except for the problem of paint. It seemed they had painted each room a different color. One room sported a very bright orange, one a robust purple, another a brilliant red and so on.

When we suggested they repaint, they refused because they had already moved out. We had to hire someone to come in and it took between three and four coats of the new neutral colored paint to cover the deep colors they had used. We deducted the cost from their security deposit, leaving the tenants very unhappy, and lots of unpleasant phone calls for me.

It's always a good idea to put a clause in the lease that lets the tenant know that they cannot make any alterations (including painting) to the house or construct any building or make any other improvements without your prior written consent. We have found this to be very helpful years later.

In another similar example, when our tenant moved out we found the once beautifully painted home now showcased a master bedroom painted solid black, including the wood trim and ceiling. We pointed out that this was not approved through us and would need to be fixed. We gave the tenant an extra week with no rent fee to put the room back to it's original color or some other neutral shade. He was very upset and did not feel he should be held accountable for repainting the room. Consequently we found the room painted a stark white with sloppily applied paint covering the wood trim.

When it comes to painting our rentals we now put a clause in the lease, and we let new tenants know we do not want them to paint without consulting us first and agreeing on the paint colors.

Checklist

⌂ Do you have a provision in the lease regarding paint?

⌂ Have you discussed the paint provision with your new tenant?

Chapter 6

Oh the Things You Will See

As a landlord you will have many interesting experiences. You may get tenants who have never previously owned or rented a house. You may have tenants who are inexperienced and/or need a little more hand holding. This doesn't mean they won't be good tenants. Knowing in advance that you need to help them along from time-to-time, however, is helpful. Even seasoned renters may require special assistance occasionally. If they offer to fix things in exchange for rent, be sure to get the receipts. You also should make sure they have the expertise or have friends who are professionals to do the work.

The day after a new tenant moved in, she called to say the garage door opener did not work. "Press the large button," I told her. The garage door opener had three buttons: two small ones on top and a much larger one underneath.

"I tried," she informed me, "but I can't get it to work."

Worried we'd have to replace the garage door opener, and wanting to show the new tenant we were responsible landlords, I felt the need to respond quickly. "I'll be right over," I said. I dropped what I was doing and quickly hopped in my car and drove to the house.

When I arrived on the spot the tenant handed me the garage door opener. I hit the large button and up the door went! "Oh, that button," she exclaimed.

"It's going to be a long year," I thought to myself.

Another tenant called the day after moving in. "There is a problem with the garbage disposal," he said.

Generally we do not check to make sure all appliances are working when a tenant moves out. We assume if something is broken they will have already told us. So, when the call came we were quick to respond. "What is it doing?" I asked.

"It won't run and it spits up food when we run the dishwasher," came the response. I knew I needed to take care of the problem quickly and sent the plumber over immediately.

Sixty dollars later, I was told by the plumber that the tenants did not know how to turn on the garbage disposal and could not find where the switch was located. The plumber also kindly informed them that they would need to run the disposal prior to using the dishwasher, or garbage would come back up.

We make it a point now to show new tenants where the garbage disposal switch is - a much less expensive strategy than hiring an emergency plumber!

A friend of mine often acts as a handyman for some of the landlords around the lakes where we live. One particular landlord was having trouble with a tenant who would wake him in the middle of the night every couple of months. It seems the tenant frequently enjoyed a night on the town but would often loose his keys. Having tired of driving over to let his tenant in at 2 am, the landlord decided to hire my friend to do it for him. After the landlord paid my friend several times, however, he suddenly stopped calling. Either it became too costly for the landlord, or the tenant decided to hide a key somewhere.

Renting out a room in your home can be a great option for generating a little additional income. Listen to this story, however, left by a landlord on an MSN message board:

"We recently bought a new house that was a little out of our league, but being that it was four bedrooms, we figured we could rent out a room for some help with the mortgage, and so we did. We found a tenant who was single, didn't drink, didn't smoke and didn't do drugs. He had a cat but said it would stay in the room (I'm allergic). So we accepted him. Long story short, his cat ran around the house, scratched my dog and the furniture, and he did drink, and he did do drugs. The one thing he never did: pay his rent on time. Oh, yeah, and he was married. One day, his estranged wife came to town with a one-way ticket and moved in with no money and a drug problem. Lo and behold, while we were out working all day, she was snooping around the house . . . "collecting" things. First, the boat hitch was missing, and then my shoes. We logged on to our banking account one day and saw there was a check made out to cash, not in our handwriting (and "dollars" was spelled wrong), with the wife's account number and signature on the back. Needless to say, we evicted them immediately and discovered she had half my wardrobe, and I am still finding things missing!" **-- Tahoe Tessy**

Although this is a very unusual case, it shows that the rental business is full of surprises!

A lovely young couple had moved in with the help of some friends and family. One of the kindly helpers suggested there might be a problem with the electricity and offered to help out. He informed them that a number of the outlets should be replaced and that he would be happy to do this for them, as he was a handyman with plenty of experience on this type of project.

The new tenants asked if this was OK. Although we had never had any complaints regarding the electric outlets and everything seemed to be working just fine when we last checked, we agreed to let him switch out a couple of receptacles.

A few weeks later the tenant called us to say that their lights were flickering from time-to-time and wondered if there were other electrical problems. We were surprised since before they moved in we'd never had a complaint about the electricity. The electric company was called and upon checking their wires could find no problem. We then went over ourselves and checked out most of the electric outlets and the electrical box. We discussed the problem with several electricians, yet could find no explanation.

One Friday night as we were getting ready to head out on vacation we received a call that the tenant's new CD player had shorted out because of electrical problems!

We postponed our trip and headed over to the house to solve the problem. We contacted a few electricians we knew and were told it might cost as much as $1200 to check out and fix the problem. This time every outlet in the house was checked, and low and behold we found the culprit. The helpful friend had incorrectly crossed the wires in one of the outlets he had replaced.

The lesson here is that while you can save money by having your tenants or their friends fix things for you, make sure that person is licensed or knows what they are doing. If not, it could cost you a lot more than you save!

Checklist

What is/will be your policy regarding minor repairs/major repairs?

Will you show your tenants where all the "secret" switches are?

Do you have a clause in your lease regarding renter repairs?

Are you prepared for the unexpected?

Chapter 7

Extracting the Rent

There have been a few times when I needed to collect rent from a tenant who was behind. Because this is an unpleasant thing to do, many landlords will hold off and let a tenant slide for some time. I recommend contacting a tenant right away if they are late. The more time that slips by the more difficult it can be to finally collect. The eviction process takes a long time and can be very costly in legal fees and lost rent. And tenants being evicted may grow angry over time and damage the home. So often I've heard from landlords that they take pity on the tenants because of their circumstances. Unfortunately the tenants did not take pity on the landlords, who lost out in the end.

When one particular tenant of ours got behind by more than a few weeks, the words of an old friend and very wise woman came back to me... "if they haven't paid the rent, call them once. If you still haven't received rent, show up on their doorstep. And keep showing up until they have paid. If you don't, you may never collect!" I took her advice and showed up at the house after my first phone call a few days earlier provided lots of excuses but no rent.

The tenant answered the door, but opened it only a crack. When he saw it was me he squeezed himself out of the door, closing it quickly behind him. The fact that he was hiding something signaled to me that the situation wasn't good.

The tenant finally left owing several weeks of rent, but it could have been worse. I always give a tenant the option of leaving if they can't afford the rent any longer. I understand that situations change. I know that if they can't afford the rent, it's better to cut your losses sooner rather than later. You can spend a lot of money and time trying to get a tenant to leave.

When a friend of mine wanted to move in with her boyfriend, she decided to rent out her home. Although inexperienced as a landlord, she wanted to be diligent in her search for a tenant. One prospect was a couple with children. My friend made the appropriate calls to their references and previous landlords, all of which resulted in glowing reviews. But two months into their lease they started to slip in the rent payments. Being the understanding person she is, my friend let them slide. The following month they became further behind. They begged for compassion and leniency as they had small children. She continued to call them about the rent, but soon they were a full four months behind. Finally she asked them to leave. They refused. She took them to court to have them evicted. Because they had children, the court was not eager to throw them out. It took six more months before the courts made them go. When she finally got possession of her house, she found it in shambles. The refrigerator was full of rotten food; garbage was everywhere. There was serious damage throughout. So not only did it cost her ten months of lost rent (she was still making house payments the entire time), it also cost her a ton of money in repairs and days of cleaning.

Long after they were gone she met someone who knew the family. That was when she learned that the references they had given her were from their own family members. In the end, my friend's kindhearted and trusting character cost her considerably.

When a tenant gets behind, make sure to find out why as soon as possible. Remember, there may be a good reason why the check hasn't turned up yet. And be reasonable. However if you sense they may not be able to afford the place, you are better off letting them out of their lease early and without penalty. It's better to have them leave on good terms. If they refuse to pay or move, start the legal process quickly. Remember it will take a long time. Again, if you can get them to move out on their own sooner, it could save you headaches, heartaches and lots of money down the road.

Checklist

☐ Do you have a plan for when a tenant can't pay?

☐ Do you have enough money to cover your expenses including mortgage payments for several months if your tenants don't pay and you need to go through the eviction process?

☐ Will you remember to be respectful of the tenant if there is a problem with paying the rent?

Chapter 8

In a Land Far Away

Renting out property that is far from where you live is a tough thing to do. How can you show the rental property to potential tenants? How do you know if the property is being kept up or run down? What will you do if your tenants don't pay their rent? How will you handle repairs and emergencies? If the property is out of state, you may also encounter higher homeowner's insurance, mortgage interest rates and down payment. And if your rental is out of state you may need to pay state taxes in two states. If you do decide to rent a property that is far from home, I highly recommend you get a management company to oversee it for you.

One landlord I know rented some property long distance for a few years without actually seeing it. When she finally traveled back to visit the rental, she discovered the shrubs had become extremely overgrown. It was terribly expensive to have them trimmed back because it had been let go for so long.

When we temporarily moved to another state, we were unable to find a house that suited us right away. We did find a duplex, however, that was very exciting to us. So we bought the property, moved in to one side and rented out the other side. Because the rent covered our payments, this arrangement worked well while we were there. It was easy enough to rent out the duplex, but when we decided to return to our home state we realized the challenges that an out-of-state landlord faces.

At first we were fortunate to have one tenant who stayed for seven years, always paid her rent on time and never caused any problems. But one day she called to say she was moving out. "Why?" I asked. She wouldn't say, other than that she had found another place. She also informed me that the young man living in the other unit was gone, and we might want to check it out.

At that point we had a management company overseeing the property for us. They found tenants and hired someone to clean or make repairs when necessary. We paid for all expenses plus repairs, and we paid the company 18 percent of the rent for their services.

After hearing from my long time tenant I quickly called the management company. They sent someone to inspect and discovered the other tenant was gone - missing perhaps. All of his belongings were still there as far as they could tell. The windows were broken and several cats had been coming in and out through the broken windows.

Some of the walls had holes in them about the size of a fist. Clothing and other belongings were thrown about everywhere. The unit was such a mess and the smell from the cats was so bad the management company had a difficult time finding anyone to clean it.

And the tenant who had been there for so long, never complaining, always paying rent on time? Well when she left we noticed how worn out the unit had become. It was in dire need of new carpet, flooring and paint throughout. It also needed new appliances. All these expenses came at the same time and it took a large part of our savings account to fix everything.

We realized an important lesson from this. It is not easy to rent property when you are far away. You need to actually see your property to know its condition. It is much easier to make the repairs year-by-year than it is to pay for everything all at once.

Checklist

Do you have someone checking on your property if it is located far from your home?

Do you have someone showing the house to prospective tenants and collecting the rent?

Have you checked into the cost of a management company? Can you afford a management company?

If you hire a Property Manager, how often do they check on the property?

Chapter 9

Welcome to the Neighborhood

When you purchase your investment property you will spend a lot of time researching the area, local rent prices, the repairs that need to be done to the property, the ability to provide a positive cash flow, and many other important matters. The one thing you probably will not or cannot check on is the neighbors. It may seem unimportant but can sometimes be a deal breaker.

The adorable little cottage with the vaulted ceiling and skylights was a great little home to show. At least most of the time. However one bright sunny day I arrived early to show the house to some excellent potential renters.

As I waited, I decided to walk around the house. I observed the large dog fenced in on one side. Although he seemed friendly enough, the smell coming from his yard was atrocious. Then the barking began. I kept my fingers crossed that the prospective tenant wouldn't want to spend much time in the back yard. I moved to the other side of the house where the driveway was situated very close to the next door neighbor's home. On the porch in rocking chairs sat the couple next door, rocking and staring. I said, "hi," and smiled at them but received a cold stare in response. I was suddenly distracted by loud music and drunken laughter coming from across the street. Three men were playing Frisbee, laughing loudly with their beer and cigarettes in hand.

One fell down and more laughter followed. It was clear they were intoxicated. It was 10 am. I could only imagine what the prospective tenants would think.

There are some things you can't fix or change. If you are purchasing real estate, you may want to consider the surrounding homes and neighbors. If you already own a property, consider the best time of day for showing the home.

We own a lovely small house in a wonderful neighborhood in a town adjacent to ours. While our house is small, the other homes are much larger and their occupants have always been exceptionally friendly to us and our tenants. One day after our tenant moved out we discovered that there were new neighbors living next door. We hoped they would be as nice as all the others.

I showed up one afternoon to finish up some painting, when I noticed the neighbors were putting on an addition to their house. They had a number of workers running electric saws and other equipment. Fortunately I wasn't showing the house that day. But what concerned me was that all of the workers' equipment was plugged into a power strip, that was plugged into an outside outlet at *our* house! When I confronted them on the matter they informed me the new neighbor had told them to plug in to our house. He didn't think I'd mind!

Two weeks later, when the painting was done, I had an appointment to show the house. I arrived a few minutes early only to be greeted by my new neighbor's very large dog. Our driveway is located between the two houses, but I wasn't able to get out of the car for several minutes. Finally the dog left and I made it into the house. A few minutes later a young lady arrived, the prospective tenant.

The neighbor's dog appeared out of nowhere and in a true Cujo style began jumping on her car and barking loudly. I tried to shoo the dog away but finally the neighbor appeared and called him back. The young lady did not get out of her car. "I'm sorry," she said to me through her window. "I just don't think this will work out."

Yes, neighbors can create problems when trying to show a house. However it can be even worse once your tenant moves in.

We truly enjoy tenants who stay for many years. One such couple had been wonderful tenants for at least ten years. They had fixed anything that broke and made numerous improvements to the house. They never complained. At least not until the day they called to say the neighbors next door were upsetting them. They'd had a fight with the people on one side of the house and asked us to intervene. "They want to put up a fence," they informed us, "right on the property line. You've got to get over here and do something!"

Now there is nothing one can do if your next door neighbor puts up a fence on their own property. We arrived at the house and tried to assure our tenants that if the neighbors put the fence up illegally we'd contact the authorities. But that did little to ease their woes.

Then they took us to their bedroom and showed us the large "No Trespassing" sign that was glaring just outside their window. It had been nailed to a tree only a few feet away. I couldn't blame them for being upset. It took up a large portion of the view and your eyes were pulled to it like a magnet.

The saga went on for some time, until our wonderful, long-standing tenants decided to move out and buy their own home. While some problems are easier to fix than others, getting a neighbor to move out of their own home is impossible.

A few years later another tenant moved into the same house. At first everything went well. They were great tenants, always paid on time and took excellent care of the house. But soon complaints began to surface regarding their neighbors. It seemed there had been a fight.

After that there were many calls and complaints with what seemed to me the expectation that we should somehow get rid of the neighbors. I knew that these neighbors were nosy. I'd seen that whenever I was working on the house between tenants. But what can you actually do about neighbors? The fighting went on until the tenants finally moved out at the end of their lease.

Yes, landlords can encounter some difficult neighbors, just like you can whenever you buy a house. There isn't much you can do about neighbors once you've made your purchase. But if you are investing in real estate for income purposes, you may want to put some consideration into the neighborhood.

Checklist

⌂ Have you met any of the neighbors at your rental property?

⌂ How would you handle any of these situations if you were the landlord?

Chapter 10

Keep the Door Open, and the Conversation Going

Staying in touch with your tenants is a good way to find out in advance if there are any issues with the property. You may also learn whether they are planning to move after their lease expires or if they will be signing a new lease. Additionally, staying in touch may help you keep good tenants longer. If your tenants know you care about the property and want it to remain in good condition for them, they will be more likely to take care of it and want to stay longer.

If your tenants call with a problem, answer their call immediately. No one likes to feel they are being ignored or neglected. If they have a problem, make sure you fix it as soon as possible, and keep them "in the loop" regarding the repairs. And an occasional, friendly "Hi, how are things going," can be helpful too. You want to know if there is a problem sooner rather than later. By keeping in contact you also may be able to prevent a future problem.

It had been over a week since I'd heard from a tenant who was getting further and further behind in his rent. I put in a call to him, but no one answered. After the second try I decided I'd better pay him a visit.

When I arrived at the house it looked different. There were no cars and it seemed like something was missing.

I knocked on the door but there was no answer. Making my way through the snow, I walked around the house. The shed was empty; its door open. I peered in the window of the house. Trash lay on the floor but the furniture was gone. I drove home to get the spare set of keys.

Later that day, upon our inspection, we found the house to be completely empty except for the piles of trash left in each room. There were holes in the walls and one of the ceiling fans had been completely destroyed. It was bent in so many directions I wondered how it could possibly have happened. There must have been a fight of some kind. Closet doors were yanked off and thrown on the floor. And all the window treatments were gone.

But that wasn't the biggest problem. We realized there was no electricity and no gas and it was the middle of the winter. The house was freezing cold. And it was the weekend. We had to wait until Monday to get the power turned back on. But it wouldn't have mattered. We discovered the heat had been turned off for over a week.

When we were finally able to get the power back up and running we discovered the pipes were all frozen. The house was on a well and we called in the well drilling company. They came out quickly but were unable to find the well pressure tank. We didn't know where it was either. We checked the entire house including the attic. Nothing. We called in another well drilling company. They couldn't find it either.

"You'll have to dig up the yard to look for it," we were told. My husband did. Through the snow and frozen ground he dug. Nothing. We called several more well drilling companies. One of them came out and said they had installed the well several years before. However, they couldn't find the paperwork that showed the location of the tank. Finally one of the well drillers owners' remembered. "It's under the front porch," he said. And he was right.

Once we had the water restored and were in the process of fixing all the broken pipes, I contacted the sheriff. He came out to assess the damage. "It's vandalism!" I complained to him. "I want to press charges."

"When was the last time you inspected the house?" the sheriff asked. "If you haven't been inspecting the house on a very regular basis, there is no way to prove that this was done recently. It could have happened over time, and therefore cannot be considered vandalism. I'm sorry, but there is really nothing you can do here."

"But in my 20 years of renting, I've never seen anything this bad." I persisted.

"You're lucky then," was his response to me. "I've seen much worse. And if this is the worst you've experienced in 20 years, you are *very* lucky."

The newspaper article in our local paper read," Landlord prepares for cleanup of home where 88 cats were removed." I could only imagine what it must be like to clean up a house that had 88 cats living in it. Apparently the smell had been so bad that the neighbors complained to authorities. The renter had lived in the house for several years and I'm guessing the landlord hadn't been to the house during that time. It's easy to just collect the rent and not give it another thought. Yet, had this landlord visited the property, he or she would have discovered the problem and might have been able to prevent it from getting so bad.

Another landlord I know owned a student rental house. One day he received a call from the housing inspector. The inspector had found a student living in the basement of the house, which was illegal. The student had been leasing out his room to another student for a higher price than he was paying and making a little extra money on the side.

The landlord went to the house to see for himself and not only found the tenant living in the basement, but found that the student had built an incredible water fountain down there!

When the temperatures were expected to dip down below zero for several days, I decided to contact my tenants and remind them to make sure the heat tape was plugged in and to let the water drip from the faucet just to make sure the pipes didn't freeze. Although I had discussed this with them when they moved in, I suspected they might not remember months later when the severe winter weather set in. Fortunately they were on top of it. The friendly reminder, however, was an excellent opportunity to keep in touch and to show me that they were taking care of the house.

It is important to keep in mind that even though things are going smoothly and you are collecting your rent on time, you still need to check on your properties. Although I don't like to intrude on my tenants, if I don't ever examine the premises I may discover problems far too late. By staying in contact with your tenants, you let them know that you are an attentive landlord, both to their needs and your own interests!

🏠 Do you have a regular schedule for inspecting the house?

🏠 Do you have a plan for keeping in touch with your tenants, calling, E-mailing or stopping by?

Chapter 11

Awesome Animal Adventures

Pets are always a big concern for landlords. Should you or shouldn't you rent to people with pets? What type of pets are OK? These are questions all landlords must decide for themselves. There are many responsible pet owners who make excellent tenants. However you may want to consider some experiences we and other landlords have experienced before you make your own decision.

Early on we rented to some tenants who had birds. We assumed that the birds would be OK. Why should we think otherwise? Birds stay in a cage. What harm could they cause, we thought? The tenants moved out at the end of their lease and we did a quick inspection. Everything looked fine on the surface. What we didn't know was that apparently the birds were permitted to fly free around the house from time-to-time. When we went back and had a closer look (having already refunded the deposit), we found lovely bird droppings on the curtain rods and behind the curtains, not to mention a number of peck marks on the windowsills.

When a potential renter calls to inquire whether you accept dogs, you will most likely want to know the size, breed and if it is housebroken. Please note: all prospective tenants have housebroken dogs. I recommend you also ask the age and weight of the animal. According to most would-be tenants a small dog weighs 65 lbs and up. Their medium sized dog may very well be a black lab weighing 150 lbs, and their large dog is probably taller than you.

I had one experience in which I agreed to allow a medium sized, well trained and housebroken dog. After signing the lease, the new tenant brought the dog into the house to meet me. The dog greeted me by wagging his tail and then lifting his leg to urinate on the carpet! At this point, unfortunately for me, it was too late. When that tenant moved out, I discovered dog hair everywhere: in the drapes, registers and every corner of the house. The smell was so horrible I felt bad for the guys who had to replace the carpeting!

I once met another landlord who told me he'd one time rented to a couple of young girls - college students. The girls had gotten a couple of large dogs "for protection," they'd told him. They soon fell behind in their rent and stopped mowing the lawn. He made several attempts to contact them. They refused to take his calls, answer the door or respond to his letters and notices.

One day he discovered a problem with the house that would require some repairs. But the presence of the dogs impeded his ability to get the job done fully, enough to avoid additional damages.

The girls finally moved out leaving behind a wake of destruction and debris. It took him several months to make it rentable again. Not only did he lose months of rent, but the damage caused far exceeded the security deposit.

You might also consider the real estate agent who was getting married. She decided to lease out her condo since she would be moving in with her new husband. She was delighted to find some great prospective tenants. They were well dressed and seemed perfect in every way. She carefully checked their credit, employment history and references. They checked out flawlessly and she was happy to rent to them. A couple of months after they moved in she stopped by to see how they were doing. She wasn't allowed in, so a few weeks later she tried calling them to make an appointment to visit. They refused. As it turned out, they had two Doberman Pincher dogs living with them. Nothing had been mentioned about owning dogs and there was nothing in the lease regarding pets. When the couple finally moved out, the woman discovered the dogs had shredded the curtains, chewed up the carpeting and clawed and scratched all the woodwork in the house, including the wood floors.

As you decide whether or not to allow pets, consider this. In every state in the USA you will find plenty of court cases where a tenant's dog has bitten someone and the landlord was sued. Rental real estate laws vary from state to state and it is very important to know the specific laws in your state. For example, after a landmark case in the State of Maryland where a young boy was mauled and nearly killed and the landlord sued, the law was changed regarding a landlord's liability in permitting certain breeds of dogs.

In 2010 there was a case in Los Angeles, California, where a postal worker was attacked by a large dog. Although the postal worker was not bitten, he was injured when he fell while attempting to protect himself and incurred some hefty medical bills. It was argued in court that the landlord was negligent because the gate to the fence holding the dog in was in need of repair. In addition the landlord was aware of the broken gate, yet had not made the repair. The jury found the dog owner to be 12 percent at fault and the landlord 88 percent at fault. The plaintiff was awarded $982,000.

Another landlord I know rented a house but did not agree to any pets. Six months into the lease she discovered that the tenants had a couple of cats. Being a pet owner and lover herself, the landlord permitted the animals to stay. After the tenant moved out the house was professionally cleaned and new tenants moved in. It turned out the new tenant was allergic to cat dander. More professional cleaners were brought in and the furnace had to be completely cleaned as well. In addition, a special cleaner had to be purchased and used to remove all the dander. All of this was at the expense of the "pet loving" landlord.

One young couple we rented to moved in and were very happy with their new home. Prior to their moving we had discussed pets and they informed us they had none. The lease also reflected that they had no pets and would need to have permission before they could keep any at the house. All went well until about two months after they moved in. We were called on a minor maintenance issue. While we were there making the repair, I noticed something a little odd. A leash was hanging on a hook and a dog toy was partially hidden behind a door. There was no dog, however, so I didn't say anything. But when I returned for a follow-up on the maintenance call, I discovered a very cute, very large brown Labrador puppy!

Of course they had lots of excuses and "hadn't planned on getting the dog." It was an uncomfortable and difficult situation. On the one hand, we could ask them to move out. But it is expensive and time consuming to replace tenants. There is lost rent, new renter search, cleaning, etc. We decided at that time to ask them for an additional deposit and an additional charge per month for the dog. We based the additional charge and deposit on the weight of the dog. It worked out well for both the tenants and for us.

The question of pets will definitely come up. Be sure to give it a great deal of thought. Allowing pets can be a great way to find a tenant, as many landlords won't permit them. But be sure to hold your tenants responsible for any damage the pet may cause.

Checklist

If you permit pets, what types, breeds or sizes will you allow?

Have you considered an additional charge for pets? Have you considered charging an additional deposit and/or monthly fee for pets?

Do you know the laws in your state regarding pets and landlord responsibilities?

Is there a provision for pets in your lease? Have you discussed this with your tenant before signing to make sure they understand their responsibilities?

If your tenant adds a pet even when you have a "no pet" clause, do you have a plan to handle the situation?

Chapter 12

The Friends and Family Deal

It is not uncommon to get a call from a friend or family member who would like to rent from you. But renting to friends and family can be risky. There is the potential for losing friends, angering family members or being severely taken advantage of. Friends and family members will ask and expect things of you that no other tenant would even consider. Sometimes things can be unintentionally damaged or broken. In the case of an unrelated tenant, you would expect them to replace or repair the broken item. It is far more difficult, however, to ask your family member or friend to do so.

Before renting to a friend or family member, it is vital to remember that being a landlord is your business. You should also consult your tax preparer as there may be special rules about what expenses you can deduct if you rent to family. And finally, think about how the relationship with family and friends could change if something unforeseen comes up, such as someone losing their job, having a health issue or making some poor financial decisions that may interfere with their paying the rent. Are you able and willing to cover that expense for them indefinitely? Or will you be able to have a difficult conversation with them?

A close family member of mine was asked to rent to his niece as a favor, since she was quite young and had no credit history. She was a nice young woman and he knew he'd be doing her a favor. Wanting to keep peace in the family, he complied. She very quickly fell behind in her rent. After months of lost rent and many very uncomfortable conversations, the young lady finally moved out. Family gatherings were not as pleasant after that. The niece who once looked up to her "favorite" uncle now felt uncomfortable around him. And the uncle felt a little resentment toward her and those who'd pressured him into renting to her. Saying "no" to family can be difficult. Saying "yes" can be even more problematic.

I was talking to a fellow landlord the other day who told me he'd rented out a house to a friend of his. He assumed his friend would be a good tenant as both the man and his wife were professionals and made a good living. In fact, the wife was an elected official and very much in the public eye. The pair fell behind in their rent and after a few months the landlord asked them to leave. At this point they owed over $3,000. He decided he would just let it go, writing it off as a poor decision. However after they left he received another surprise. They'd also stuck him with a $300 water bill!

On an MSN Real Estate message board, one landlord had this experience in renting to a relative.

"I had let my cousin (at the request of my aunt) move in, and she sold my water heater, air-conditioning unit, all the fixtures in the house and all my children's furniture and living-room furniture I had let her use, my riding lawn mower and anything else she could remove. Then

she left in the middle of the night. Now, two years later, she has no problem walking into any family gathering and acting like she does not understand why I do not speak with her." -- **Amalga**

If you do decide to rent to a friend or family member, it is even more important to have things spelled out in writing. Be sure to follow the same procedures as you do with any other tenant: lease, checklist and lots of discussion about your expectations - in a friendly manner of course!

Checklist

□ Do you have a rule in place regarding renting to friends and family?

□ If you rent to family or friends and there is a problem, do you have a plan for handling these situations?

Chapter 13

Who's in Your Corner?

Who do you know? Or more specifically, who do you know who is able to fix your furnace, repair your pipes, rewire your house, put on a new roof, and fix all the other problems that may arise? Having friends in the service industry is a real benefit to a landlord. While you may be able to do some of these tasks yourself, unless you want this as your full time job and you are good at all of these things, you are going to need help. I suggest you line up some talented people--people who are good at what they do, people you know and trust.

I've spoken with a number of other property managers and landlords and I believe the number one repair you will have is with plumbing. Clogged drains and toilets are very common problems for landlords.

One situation we encountered was when a tenant called with a clogged drain. We sent our plumber right over to fix the situation. He informed us that after trying everything he could, he was unable to unclog the drain. He said the tenant had been putting so much grease and food down the drain that it was backed up much too far for his equipment to handle. We then had to call in the big guys--the drain specialists with the heavy duty equipment. Talk about expensive! We ended up paying more than double the normal fee.

As sometimes happens, you hire a person to inspect the job and are unable to be there when the service person comes. So the tenant must meet with your repairman. This is when it's especially good to have someone you know and who knows you. I've had tenants ask my handyperson to make all kinds of additional changes to the house. For example, my handyman went over to make a repair to a shower head and the tenant asked him to build in an additional closet. Fortunately he asked me prior to doing the work. Another tenant wanted my plumber to replace light fixtures.

You may want the service person to speak with you directly when the tenant is not around. Once during a routine furnace inspection, the service person mentioned in front of the tenant that the furnace was a few years old and therefore could not be guaranteed. So even though he could find nothing wrong, we had to replace a perfectly fine furnace. The repair person left quite happy; our checking account not so much.

Previously I mentioned that plumbing is the most common repair for landlords. One incident that sticks out in my mind happened to a friend of mine. His tenant called him to say her child had flushed a toy down the toilet. He quickly went to investigate the situation. It was not the first time this had happened. The toilet was severely clogged and had to be completely taken apart.

In the end he discovered he'd hit the jackpot. The child had actually flushed 13 toys down the toilet!

You never know what you are going to come up against next. But without having people you can trust, who you know will charge you a fair price, you can end up spending more money than you ever imagined possible. Develop good relationships with service people. And count on the unexpected.

Checklist

Do you have a plumber you can trust?

⌂ Do you know a good electrician you can call upon?

⌂ Are you handy with repairs? Or do you have a reliable handy person who can do the work for you?

⌂ Have you prepared for the possibility of making repairs? For example, will the rent you are collecting cover the costs?

Chapter 14

Security Leaks

Tenants can be great, and everything can go well throughout the term of the lease. That is until that final day when the tenant moves out and the house needs to be inspected for damage. This is when the relationship can become strained. People always want to receive a full deposit and often it is difficult to see things from the other's point of view. There have been some situations where we've had different viewpoints from our tenants.

One incident involved missing garbage cans. The tenant insisted that those we provided were no good. So he threw them out and purchased new ones that he said now belonged to him. (The garbage cans we provided seemed fine to us when he moved in.)

In another situation a tenant was very proud of his young daughter's artwork. He covered all the living room walls with more than 100 of her paintings. When he took the artwork down it peeled the paint, and in many places, part of the drywall, leaving holes everywhere. Imagine my surprise when I saw the big beautiful living room with cathedral ceilings and more than 100 holes! Each hole had to be filled with spackle and the entire room painted. A professional painter charged an exceptionally high price to patch the job. Needless to say the tenant was very unhappy about not getting all of his deposit back.

One young couple who rented from us were very concerned about cleanliness. They insisted on having the house professionally cleaned before moving in. They wanted new carpeting as well. We replaced the carpet and they hired a cleaner. Before the year was up the couple had a big fight, were splitting up, and needed to move out. Upon inspection of the house, I discovered the bedroom door had a large two fisted hole in it, and the bathroom door was broken as well. They were very concerned about their deposit. I agreed to give them an extra week to put the house back in order. Two weeks later they were finally out. They replaced the bedroom door with one that was much less expensive than our original door. But the biggest surprise to me were the mini-mountains of garbage left behind in the living room and throughout the house. Don't assume because someone wants the house spotless when they move in, that they will leave it that way!

When you get your new tenant you will be excited about finally finding someone who seems perfect for your rental. They meet all, or at least most, of your qualifications. The new tenant is also excited about moving into a new home and you are eager to please one another. Sometimes promises are made that are later regretted.

Moving is stressful and the new tenant is so happy to have found a landing place. This will be the tenant's home and they want to be happy in their new place, and you also want them to be happy and comfortable. So you agree to let them make some changes. Usually you forget about the fact that they may or may not be able to keep those promises and put everything back to its original state when they move out. So when one of our new tenants asked to replace our brick walkway with their own walkway, we agreed.

What we forgot to consider is that when a tenant is moving out, they have a lot going on. They have a number of people helping them and they are usually in a hurry. In their haste to replace our brick walkway, the gate was broken. The bricks were left sitting on top of the ground, rather than in the ground. It looked terrible! Nothing like the nice walkway they started with. The tenant's memory of how things looked before the move-in also differs from yours. The solution can be as simple as taking a before and after photo. Sometimes a picture is worth a thousand words.

We received a call in September from some new tenants who had moved into our property in May of that year, wondering where the storm windows were. It had turned cold and they were concerned about the cost of the winter heating bills.

We asked them to check the storage shed and the attic. "We've looked everywhere," they responded. And they had. No storms could be found. It appeared that the previous tenants had moved out and thrown them away.

Now storm windows can be very costly to replace. They generally must be custom made. Talk about a great lesson! Make sure when you are going though the house to assess damage after a tenant moves out that you check for the storm windows.

We have found that many tenants have their own appliances and would prefer to use them. Why not? It's fine to allow the tenants to use their own. However your appliances will need to be stored for the duration of the lease. And someone will need to move them out and back in. You will need to decide if you want to do that or not. If you make this your tenant's responsibility, you may want to ask how and where they will store them. You want them still to be in good working condition for the next tenant.

It is always useful to have a checklist to document the original condition of the property. That way when the tenant moves out, both of you will have something to fall back on. Be sure to include agreements about appliances and alterations to the property and photos showing "before" and "after." Most checklists require the signatures of both tenant and landlord. This is the best way later on to avoid arguments as to the condition of the property.

Another good idea is to send your tenants a "moving-out" letter prior to the end of their lease. This letter will remind them of the condition in which they found the unit, the condition they agreed to leave it, the agreed upon move out date, the procedure for the final walk-through, and when they can expect to see the return of their security deposit. You may also want to include a reminder to switch the utilities back to you, complete a change of address form with the post office, and leave you a forwarding address, where you can mail their deposit.

Consider doing a preliminary walk-through to determine what if any work will be needed before you can begin showing the home to the next prospective renters. If you plan on showing the property prior to the move-out date, you can inform your tenants of your plans and ask them to help you. (Tenants should have been made aware of plans to show the property before the end of their lease prior to or when the lease is signed, and should be included in the lease.) Offering to write up a letter of recommendation for your tenants will help ensure a good transition.

Checklist

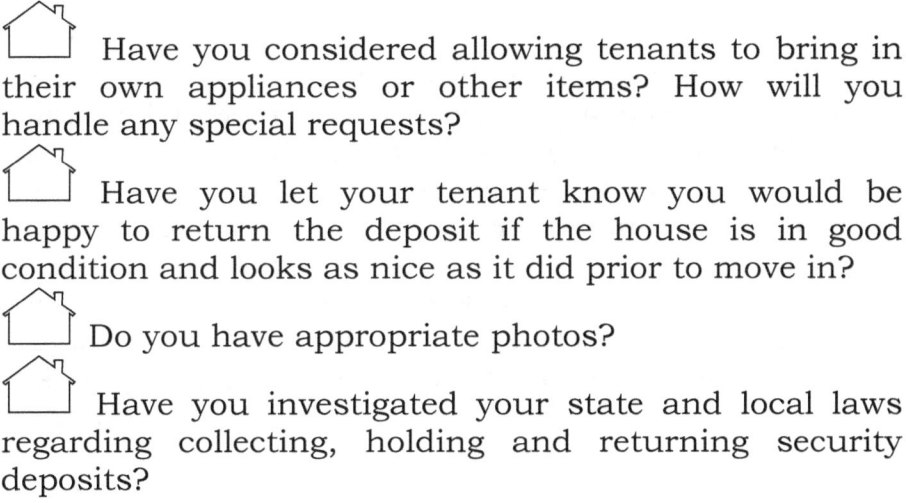

Have you considered allowing tenants to bring in their own appliances or other items? How will you handle any special requests?

Have you let your tenant know you would be happy to return the deposit if the house is in good condition and looks as nice as it did prior to move in?

Do you have appropriate photos?

Have you investigated your state and local laws regarding collecting, holding and returning security deposits?

Chapter 15

No Vacancy

Sometimes your rental property is going to be vacant. You may be in-between tenants and doing repairs or cleaning or you may be trying to sell your rental property. In any case, you should be aware of some of the hazards involved in having vacant property.

When we first started renting out houses, my husband also began managing some other rental properties. He once experienced a problem in a commercial building that also housed apartments above the stores. At one point a unit had become vacant and needed some painting and minor repairs. My husband had left some tools and his paint supplies in the apartment, and so carefully made sure he locked the place up tightly when leaving. When he returned the following day he found an extremely foul odor in the unit. He fervently looked around for the source. In one of the bedrooms, he discovered a man sleeping on the floor. Shocked, he chased the man out. It really bothered him because he couldn't figure out how the man could possibly have gotten into the second floor apartment. Later that week while talking to one of his tenants, he discovered the sleeping intruder was a friend of the renter in a unit that was near the one that was vacant. The tenant had notified his friend of the vacancy and allowed him to crawl out of his window, across a narrow ledge and in through the window of the vacant apartment. After that, my husband always remembered to lock the windows when he finished with his repairs for the day.

A story recently aired on the nightly news regarding a problem with a rental house that had just been sold. Following an extended time period of problems and lost rent from a tenant, the landlord decided to evict the tenant and sell the house. Before the new owner could take possession, the house, which had recently been remodeled and updated with new appliances, was attacked by scrappers. They got away with the new furnace and hot water heater and even took the back door! All of this was caught on video. The thieves were believed to have been assisted by the previous tenants.

I have recently heard about several cases that involve squatters or renters moving into vacant houses. In these cases the owner is unaware that this is going on at his property. In Orlando, Florida, a man was found to be renting out a vacant home to more than one person. He placed an ad on Craigslist and found a tenant. After paying the rent, the new tenant went to look at the home. She was shocked to find someone was already living there. But the biggest surprise came when she found out the "landlord" didn't even own the house! He had found the home empty and thought he'd make some quick cash.

And consider the squatters in California who had been occupying vacant property for more than a year before a judge eventually issued an eviction notice against them. Upon entering the premises the authorities found mud and dirt everywhere, pornographic images and spray painted messages, and ripped up floors throughout the property.

In another case, a Colorado couple temporarily moved to Indiana. Soon after the move, they discovered through a neighbor in Colorado that someone had moved into their locked and secured, yet vacant, Colorado home. It seems the people had purchased an "adverse possession" deed to their home for $5,000 through a real estate agent. The couple went through the eviction process to get the deed holders, who had by now been living in the home for a few months, to leave. The process takes quite a bit of time but eventually the owners won the court case to evict. The illegal deed holders discovered a loophole in the legal system and filed bankruptcy, preventing the courts or police from forcing them to leave. The case lingered on for over a year. In the meantime the couple and their two young children were living in the basement of some friends while they continued to make their mortgage payments.

There are dozens of these cases all across the United States with far too many innocent victims. Some home-owners were on vacation for only five days and came home to find a squatter had moved in, changed the locks and put up "no trespassing" signs in the windows. Many homes have been broken into and ransacked by thieves, or used for wild "rave" parties and vandalized. Other vacant homes become a safe haven for squatters who can produce a fake lease, or even some who have become victims themselves, unaware they were renting a property illegally.

No landlord wants his property to be vacant for long. If you are doing work on it that will take several weeks, ask a neighbor to let you know if they see anything suspicious. Keep the lawn mowed and mail picked up. You could park a car in the driveway and leave lights on as well to make it appear "lived-in."

If you do incur unwelcome and/or unpaid occupants in your rental property, consult an attorney before trying to remove them yourself. In most cases it is illegal to take action on your own and a court ordered eviction may be necessary. You can contact the local police for help. However, if they are unable or unwilling to assist, you should begin legal proceedings immediately.

One more thing to note: many insurance companies will not insure a home that is vacant for more than 30-60 days, because unoccupied houses pose a higher risk for a number of problems including fire, plumbing leaks, rodents and termites. Bottom line: if your house is vacant make sure it is locked and that you and the neighbors are paying close attention to it!

Checklist

⌂ Do you know the neighbors well enough to ask them to keep an eye on your property when it is vacant?

⌂ Have you read over your insurance policy to see what kind of coverage you have when your property is vacant?

Chapter 16

Positive Notes

So far I've talked about many difficult situations and some less than pleasant experiences. I've discussed tenants who've caused many problems for landlords and alarming expenses. But there also have been many great tenants who deserve positive recognition. Many of our tenants have made wonderful improvements to our homes. We've had tenants who've added decks and patios, new sheds, new flooring, light fixtures, beautiful gardens, and many other embellishments. Most of our tenants paid every month without fail, either on time or early!

When their lease was up the tenants asked us to have a final walk-through with them. We agreed to meet that afternoon. We hadn't been to the house in a few months so did not really know what to expect. Would they point out all the flaws that had been there when they moved in, we wondered.

As we arrived we couldn't help but notice how nice the entrance looked. They had spruced it up and made it look happy. As we entered the house we went into shock. Everything looked so beautiful, clean and new. Appliances, paint, window treatments, cupboard door handles and flooring - it was beautiful!

Walking outside with them was like walking into a garden paradise. The lawn was well manicured and the flower beds had been pruned and weeded. A sandstone wall had been built all around the flower beds. We were amazed at finding the house looking so much nicer than it had when they moved in!

As you prepare to purchase and/or rent out property, keep the following in mind:

1. Remember, rental property is a business. Have a plan; do the math.
2. Make the home as appealing as you can to attract good tenants.
3. Hold out for the best tenants whenever you can, even if you start to feel desperate.
4. Make sure your lease covers all the bases.
5. Know all the laws and rules of rental real estate in your area.
6. Have a troop of professionals you can call on: attorney, plumber, electrician, heating & cooling company, and a good handyman.
7. Treat your tenants like you would want to be treated, *and expect them to hold up their end of the agreement.*

Renting property can be very rewarding and educational. You'll learn more about home repairs than you ever imagined and you'll also learn some important things about yourself.

Remember, although great tenants may sometimes be difficult to come by, they do exist. If you want to find and keep great tenants, be sure your property is clean and appealing and is in good mechanical condition. Always be respectful of your tenants *and* keep in touch with them to let them know you care - about them and about your property.

May your tenants be the finest
and your rental properties beautiful and prosperous!

Appendix A

Rental Property Business Plan Template

OWNER(S)

Address Line 1
Address Line 2
City, ST ZIP Code
Telephone
Fax
EMail

I. Table of Contents

I. **Table of Contents**

II. **Executive Summary** - Write this section last. When you have completed the rest of this document, make a bulleted outline of your plan. Be sure to show the main points.

III. **General Description** - Describe your general plan for purchasing and renting out your property. Include your own personal experience in property management, property ownership and business, previous home and/or business ownership, licenses such as plumbing, electrical, heating & cooling, contracting, business experience such as accounting, sales, customer service, etc.

IV. **Type of Rental Real Estate** - Describe the type of housing you are offering: apartment, duplex, single family dwelling, multi-family dwelling, high rent district, low income, weekly tourist, etc.

V. **Marketing** - Who is your target market? What type of tenants are you seeking to attract? Are they professionals, young families, retirees or singles? How will the property you are choosing fit the lifestyle of the target renters? How will this property appeal to your target audience? Include any marketing research you have to support your plan. How will you advertise for your renters?

Describe the unique advantages your property offers over other similar rentals in the area. Does it have an updated kitchen & bath, prime location, laundry facilities on site, attractive exterior / interior? Is it in a nice neighborhood, close to shopping, high employment area, or low crime area or private rural setting? Is there mass transportation available, lots of recreation nearby, good school system, affordable housing, etc.?

Describe the competition for similar rental properties in the area. What do they offer? How much is the rent? How does your property compare?

VI. **Operational Plan** - How will the property be leased: yearly, weekly, month-to-month? Will a lease be required?

VII. **Management and Organization** - Will a management company or property manager be appointed or will the owner manage the day-to-day operations, such as finding tenants and collecting rents. Describe how repairs will be made to the property. Will the owner make the repairs himself/herself or will someone else be hired.

VIII. **Personal Financial Statement** - Include the personal financial stats for each owner, showing assets and liabilities and personal net worth. Bankers and investors usually want to see this information.

IX. **Startup Expenses and Capitalization** - Explain how much startup investment you will be providing. Include any down payments, personal property (appliances, building materials etc. that you currently own and intend to use on the property), cash reserve for remodeling or repairs.

X. **Financial Plan** - What are the annual operating costs for this property? Include mortgage principal and interest per year, insurance, taxes for non-owner occupant, sewer fees, water fees, garbage pick-up etc.

What major repairs and remodeling are you anticipating over the next five years? Include roof, furnace, well, landscaping and tree removal, decking, updating, appliances such as hot water heater, water softener, washer/dryer, stove, refrigerator, dishwasher etc. How will these repairs be financed?

Your financial plan should include a 12-month profit and loss projection, and a cash flow projection (A four-year profit and loss projection, a projected balance sheet and a break-even calculation may also be included.) This will also help you think through your plan and show how feasible your rental property will be.

XI. **Appendices** - Include details used in your business plan including maps and photos of location, copies of leases, list of assets available as collateral for a loan, and any other documentation that supports your plan.

Appendix B

Sample Projected Profit and Loss Statement - Rental Property

Projected Profit & Loss
January 1 - December 31, 20xx

Rental Income / Expense

Income

Rental Unit #1	$13,200
($1200/mo@11 months	
1 month vacant)	

Total Income	**$13,200**

Gross Profit	$13,200

Expense

Mortgage Interest	$6,500
Other Interest	75
Homeowners Insurance	950
Real Estate Taxes	3,100
Repairs	1375
Cleaning Expense	90
Supplies	20
Legal Fees	275
Professional Fees	0
Advertising	0
Travel & Auto expense	75
Management Fees	0
Utilities	43
Garbage	150
Bank Service Charges	25

Total Expense	**$11,678**

Net Income	$522

Appendix C

Sample Cash Flow Projection

	Month	Month	Month	Month	Total Yr
Beginning Cash Balance	0	0	0	0	0
Cash Inflow (Rent collected)					
Total Cash Inflows					
Total Cash Balance					
Cash Outflows (Expenses)					
Mortgage Interest Insurance Taxes Repairs Bank Service Charges Utilities Garbage					
Subtotal Other Cash Outflows					
Total Cash Outflows					
Ending Cash Balance					

Appendix D

Stats and useful tidbits

Popular Features for Renters

Location
        Close to work, family, friends
Clean & Tidy
Renovations
        Looks new - especially kitchen & bath
Space: size of rental unit, size of bedrooms
Laundry facilities
Pets
Windows/natural light

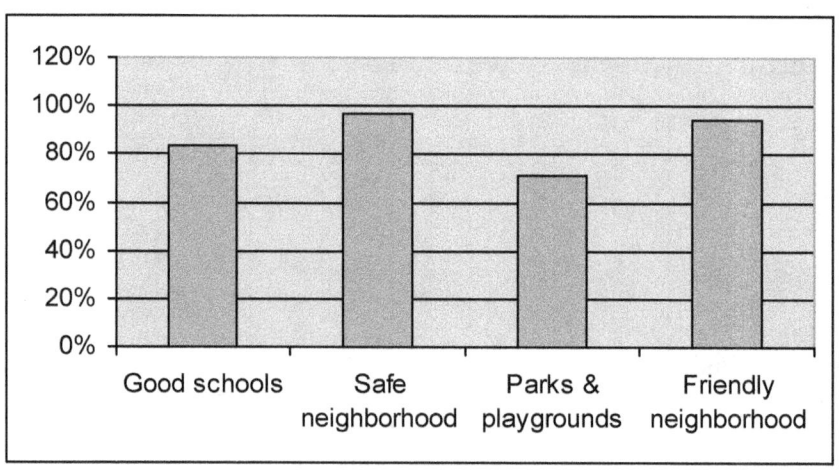

Most Common Complaints by Tenants

Poor management
      slow to make repairs
      failure to take or return phone calls
Facilities
      lack of laundry facilities
      no dishwasher
      lack of closet space
      high heating costs

Average age of renters - 20-34-year-old

Most Common Calls received by Landlords

Clogged drains
Can't pay rent on time
Bugs/mold
Locked out
Heating & Cooling problems

Most Common Complaints by Landlords

Late payments
Using security deposit as rent
Violation of rules

The Search for Rentals

90% of renters search the internet for available space
50% of apartment renters search 2-4 months in advance (house data unavailable)
17% of apartment renters search 1 month or less (house data unavailable)

About The Author

Linda and Scott Grischy began their careers as landlords 30 years ago when, having outgrown their first small home, they decided to rent it out and purchase another that would better fit their needs. It was a decision that was both a life-changing and life-learning journey for them and their family. Since that time they have bought, sold, managed and rented out houses and multi-unit properties in two different states. The lessons learned and the people met along the way have turned the journey into an ongoing and unforgettable adventure. In "What *Real* Landlords *Know*," Linda shares their adventure with you.

www.ingramcontent.com/pod-product-compliance
Lightning Source LLC
Chambersburg PA
CBHW071752170526
45167CB00003B/1003